A Girl Named

Rosa

The True Story of
ROSA PARKS

By **Denise Lewis Patrick**
Illustrated by **Melissa Manwill**

Scholastic Inc.

Published by Scholastic Inc., *Publishers since* 1920. SCHOLASTIC and associated logos are trademarks and/or registered trademarks of Scholastic Inc. The publisher does not have any control over and does not assume any responsibility for author or third-party websites or their content.

The story on pages 47–48 first appeared in *American Girl* magazine in the Sept/Oct 2016 issue.

Photos ©: 43: The Granger Collection; 44 top left: The Granger Collection; 44 top right: The Granger Collection; 44 center right: Universal History Archive/Getty Images; 45 center: Don Cravens/Getty Images; 45 bottom: Underwood Archives/Getty Images; 46 top: Jeff Kowalsky/AFP/Getty Images; 46 bottom: David Coates/AP Images; 47: Andrea Cipriani Mecchi.

Book design by Suzanne M. LaGasa
Special thanks to Dr. Felicia Bell

Library of Congress Cataloging-in-Publication Data available

ISBN 978-1-338-19307-7

10 9 8 7 6 5 4 3 2 1   18 19 20 21 22

Printed in the U.S.A.   23
First printing 2018

Contents

Introduction

How does a small brown-skinned girl growing up in a tiny town in Alabama become a woman who is known all over the world? Rosa Parks stood up for fairness and equality by sitting down on a bus in Montgomery, Alabama, in 1955. Her simple act helped change laws all over America.

Rosa was a brave little girl who grew up to make a big difference.

Chapter 1

A Place Called Pine Level

Rosa Louise McCauley was born in Tuskegee, Alabama, on February 4, 1913. Her mother, Leona, was a teacher. Her father, James, built houses. When Rosa was only two and her brother, Sylvester, was a baby, their father left to find better work. Rosa, her mother, and brother moved to Pine Level, Alabama, to live with her grandparents.

Pine Level was a small **community**. Many people, like Rosa's grandfather, owned or worked on farms. Her uncle was a **minister**. Going to church became a favorite and important part of Rosa's life.

Rosa's parents separated, and her father never came back to live with the family. Her mother had to get a new teaching job.

The school was in another town, too far away from Pine Level for her to travel back and forth every day. She was only able to spend weekends with Rosa and Sylvester.

Rosa loved spending time with her grandparents. They went fishing together. She learned to plant corn and milk cows from her grandfather. Rosa's grandmother taught her how to cook, sew, and make quilts.

And although Rosa's grandparents taught her to *do* many things, they also helped her understand that their lives were very different from the lives of their white neighbors.

ATS
OPEN
HOMEMADE
STRUDELS & PASTRIES
HELP WANTED
WHITE ONLY

Chapter 2

Lessons in Being Brave

One of the most important lessons Rosa learned from her grandparents was about how to respect herself even when others didn't. Many white people didn't want African Americans to have equal rights. In some states, there were laws to keep black people separate from whites. They didn't want African Americans to vote to change those laws.

These laws told black people where they could live, shop, or sit in the movies. There were separate hospitals for black and white people, and in some states white nurses could not treat black patients. Black people weren't

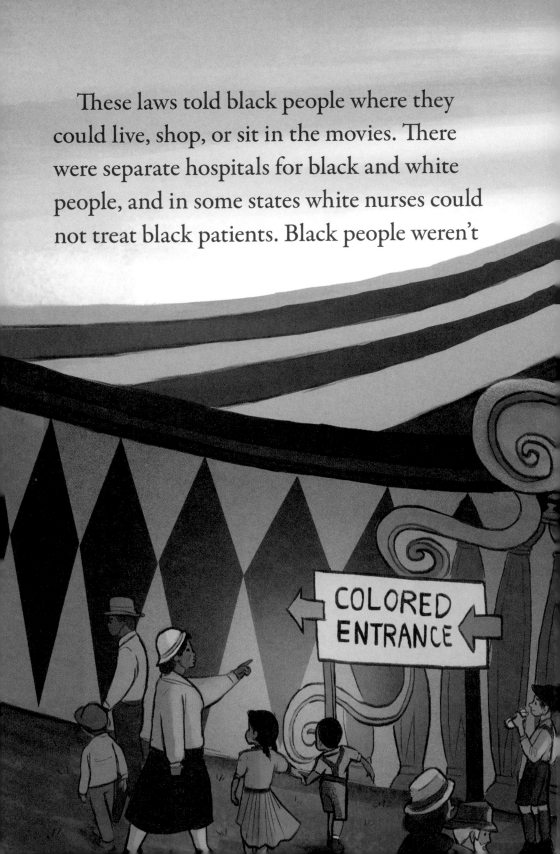

COLORED
ENTRANCE

allowed to walk into places through the same entrance as white people, not even into the circus.

Across the country, there were white groups who used violence to frighten, and sometimes hurt, black people. In Rosa's community, gangs of white men wearing robes and masks sometimes attacked black people, setting fire to their churches, schools, and homes.

The violence got so bad that many people did not feel safe. When Rosa was five or six years old, her aunt and cousins stayed at her grandparents' house every night. They boarded up their windows so that no one could break in. The family kept their clothes on in case they had to escape quickly.

Rosa's grandfather sat up all night to protect his family. Rosa sometimes sat with him. His bravery taught her to not be afraid of the dangers or hardships she might face in everyday life.

Chapter 3

Leaving Home to Learn

Rosa learned to read and count before she started school. When she was six, she went to the black elementary school in Pine Level. There was one teacher for all the grades. The white elementary school had a different teacher for each grade.

Rosa and the other black children had to walk to school, no matter how far away they lived. The white children got to ride on a school bus. Sometimes the white children threw things at Rosa and her friends from the bus windows. They had to duck and jump into the ditch to avoid getting hit.

Many black children in the South only went to school for a few months out of the year because they had to work during planting and **harvest** time. Rosa and her cousins picked cotton alongside the grown-ups in their family, earning only a few cents each day. Rosa was proud of the hard work she could do, but she longed to go back to school.

When Rosa was ready for junior high, there was no black junior high or high school in town. Her mother made a big decision and sent Rosa away to Montgomery Industrial School. The school was more than twenty miles away, so Rosa had to live with relatives in Montgomery.

At Rosa's new school, all the girls were black. All the teachers, including Miss Alice White who started the school, were white. Rosa had never had a white teacher before, but she didn't mind.

She was excited to study math and science. Like many girls in the 1920s (no matter what race), Rosa also learned how to knit and how to take care of a home.

Rosa began dreaming of her future. She started making plans to stay in Montgomery and continue her education.

Chapter 4

Black and White

Everywhere Rosa looked, things were **segregated**, or separated, for black and white people. Black people had to use different bathrooms. They had to use different water fountains. Rosa wondered if the water in white fountains tasted different somehow.

Even though things weren't fair, Rosa always obeyed the laws and didn't start any trouble— until once, when she was walking along a Montgomery street.

A white boy tried to knock her down. Rosa shoved him back. He told his mother, who was standing nearby. Even after Rosa tried to explain, the mother threatened to have Rosa

put in jail. Luckily, that didn't happen.

As Rosa grew older, she worked hard to keep **racism** from making her act out in anger again.

Chapter 5

Getting Involved

Although Rosa wanted to finish high school, she had to drop out to take care of her grandparents and her mother. In between caring for them, she worked many different jobs. When Rosa was eighteen, a friend introduced her to Raymond Parks.

Rosa and Raymond married in 1932. He encouraged Rosa to complete high school, and she did!

Raymond Parks also encouraged Rosa to get involved in the **civil rights** movement. He was a member of the National Association for the Advancement of Colored People (NAACP). This organization had been formed by a group of black and white people who wanted to end unfair laws.

Rosa Parks became a leader of the Youth Council of the Montgomery NAACP in 1949. She wanted to give young black girls and boys what her grandfather had given her—courage and a sense of self-respect.

Those qualities helped Rosa deal with the unjust laws that existed in many states.

One type of unfair law that the black people
in Montgomery faced every day was about
public transportation. On city buses, white
riders sat at the front, and a certain number of
seats at the back were allowed for black riders.

Black people had to pay in front, then get off and walk to the rear door of the bus to get on. Sometimes drivers let black riders pay, and then pulled away before they could get to the back door.

If all the back seats were taken, black riders had to stand—even if there were empty seats in front. Anyone who broke the rules—or tried to—was arrested.

Chapter 6

A Serious Choice

On Thursday, December 1, 1955, Rosa Parks waited for the bus after work. She paid her fare and then went to enter the back door to the black section. She got a seat in a row with two other black people. The bus became crowded, and the white section was full. The driver told the black people to get up because there was a white man standing in the aisle.

The two people next to Rosa moved. She decided not to give up her seat. She wasn't simply tired from work that day. She was tired of all the times she'd been treated unfairly. She made a serious choice. The driver refused to move the bus. Rosa refused to move herself. He called the police.

Forty-two-year-old Rosa was arrested and taken to jail because she would not give up her seat on a city bus. She was released from jail later that night. No one, not even Rosa, imagined what would happen in Montgomery after that day.

Word spread across the black community in Montgomery about what Rosa had done.

They decided they'd had enough. They decided to protest by not riding the buses. Instead, they would **boycott** the buses— many people walked wherever they had to go. Others got rides from black and white friends who drove cars.

On Monday morning, December 5, as Rosa Parks went before a judge, Montgomery city buses were empty of black passengers. They were empty the day after, too, and for weeks after. News of the boycott, and pictures of Rosa Parks, spread throughout the United States, and the world. The boycott lasted for thirteen months.

In December 1956, the city of Montgomery ended bus segregation and the boycott ended.

The Parks family moved to Detroit, Michigan, where they continued to be active in the civil rights movement.

Rosa's firm belief in fighting nonviolently for civil rights never ended. That brave girl became a strong, courageous woman who spent the rest of her life traveling, speaking, and standing up for equality.

GLOSSARY

BOYCOTT: to refuse to take part in something as a way of making a protest

CIVIL RIGHTS: the rights that all people have for equal treatment under the law

COMMUNITY: a group of people who live in the same area or have something in common with each other

HARVEST: the collection or gathering of crops that are ripe

MINISTER: a person who is authorized to lead religious ceremonies in a church

RACISM: the belief that a particular race is better than others

SEGREGATE: the practice of keeping people or groups apart

TIMELINE

1913: Rosa Louise McCauley is born in Tuskegee, Alabama, on February 4

1915: Rosa's baby brother, Sylvester, is born on August 20

1917: Rosa, her brother, and mother move to Pine Level, Alabama, to live with her grandparents

1919: Rosa starts attending Pine Level Elementary School

A teacher and African American students in front of a schoolhouse, in the south, circa 1920

1924: Rosa starts attending Montgomery Industrial School

Raymond Parks, circa 1947

A young Rosa Parks, circa 1935

Rosa Parks's mug shot after she was arrested

1932: Rosa marries Raymond Parks

1933: Rosa receives her high school diploma at age 20

1949: Rosa becomes a leader of the Youth Council of the Montgomery NAACP

1955: Rosa is arrested for refusing to give up her seat to a white man on a city bus on December 1; Montgomery bus boycott begins

1956: Montgomery bus boycott and bus segregation ends

1957: Rosa and her family move to Detroit, Michigan

1960: President Eisenhower signs the Civil Rights Act of 1960 into law

RIGHT: African American commuters walking to work instead of riding the buses during the Montgomery bus boycott, 1956

BELOW: Rosa Parks riding a bus in Montgomery in 1956

1999: Rosa receives Congressional Gold Medal

2000: Rosa Parks Library and Museum opens at Troy University in Montgomery, on the site where she was arrested in 1955

Rosa Parks receiving the Congressional Gold Medal in 1999

2005: Rosa Parks dies at the age of ninety-two on October 24

2013: A postage stamp with Rosa's picture is released on Feburary 4, her 100th birthday

Unveiling of the Rosa Parks 100th birthday commemorative postage stamp at the Charles H. Wright Museum of African American History in Detroit, Michigan

A GIRL NAMED MARLEY

There are a lot of young girls helping to make positive changes in our world today, just like Rosa Parks did. Marley Dias is one of those girls.

Marley noticed that something major was missing from the books she was reading in school. "I wasn't seeing girls like me—black girls who are smart," she says. In fact, most of the stories her class was reading in school didn't feature any characters at all who were black. "The ones that did were very one-dimensional. Black girls are not being portrayed fully," Marley explains.

So the New Jersey girl, then eleven years old, set out to collect one thousand amazing stories featuring black girls. "Black girls need to see stories about girls like them," Marley says. "Our voices and stories are so important." She created the hashtag #1000blackgirlbooks, and her book drive took off. Marley began receiving books from people all over the world. She has collected more than 9,000 books of many different genres.

Marley decided to donate the books to a school in Jamaica, where her mom is from. "We delivered the books in person," Marley says. "I think it's important to step out of your comfort zone." Marley is still collecting books and speaking about the importance of black female characters. "You don't have to be the best," she says. "You just have to do your best and do what you love."

Look for Marley's book: *Marley Dias Gets It Done (And So Can You!)* published by Scholastic Press.